GERBILS

Keith Lawrence BVSc, MRCVS

Hamlyn

London · New York · Sydney · Toronto

Introduction

Gerbils originate from the desert regions of Asia and North Africa. It is only as recently as the early 1950s that they were generally available in the USA, and they were unknown as pets in the UK until 1964. Now, however, they have become one of the most widely kept pets, perhaps because of their appealing natures.

Gerbils are small, desert animals. They often balance on their hind legs to inspect their surroundings curiously.

In many ways the gerbil is the ideal small pet. Unlike hamsters, which are nocturnal, gerbils are active for short periods throughout the day. They are friendly, alert, curious and easy to tame. They are also odourless and, because they were originally desert animals, they conserve moisture by producing very little urine and hard dry faeces.

In the wild, gerbils live in underground tunnels and your pet will also dig burrows in its cage. They often balance themselves on their hind legs to examine their surroundings and free their front paws to hold food such as seeds. Their long hind legs also enable them to leap away from enemies, but when running they normally drop on to all fours.

The male tends to be larger than the female and weighs on average 130g (4½oz) compared to an average weight of 70g (2½oz) for the female.

The average life span is about three years, although with careful attention to diet and general cleanliness, some may live for up to five years. Gerbils do not hibernate although they have a tendency to sleep for long periods if the room temperature becomes too high. They make little if any noise but when alarmed will drum the ground with their hind legs.

Wild gerbils are sandy brown, and so are most pet gerbils. Few variations are available because the period of domestication has been too short.

Choosing and buying

By their nature, gerbils are highly gregarious and a solitary gerbil is likely to be very unhappy unless it receives a lot of attention from its owner. It is much better to buy a pair of young gerbils to keep each other company. A couple from the same community litter should be compatible: do not bring together two strange adults as there will almost inevitably be a serious fight.

Both sexes make good pets but think very carefully before obtaining a male and a female since these small animals are prolific breeders.

It is best to buy gerbils when they are 4-6 weeks old, by which time they will have been weaned. Healthy gerbils are usually alert, interested in their surroundings and full of curiosity. They will move quickly and freely about their cages. On no account should you buy a timid individual.

Before buying your pet, check the points in the following table.

Signs of Health
Head
Nose It should be clean, free of mucous, blemishes and other discharges.

Eyes They should be clean and bright with no discharges. Check for prominence of the third eyelid. Ensure there is no wetness around the eyes.

Teeth The incisors should be growing parallel and should not be overlong. They should not be visible when the mouth is closed.

Ears They should be covered with hair, and free from scabs and waxy discharge.

Body

Coat The coat should be smooth and glossy with no areas of hair loss, sores or wounds.

Feet Make sure there are no missing or damaged claws.

Anus Make sure the area under the tail is clean and unstained. Staining usually means diarrhoea.

Your pet gerbil will quickly overcome its timidity and approach to take a titbit from your hand.

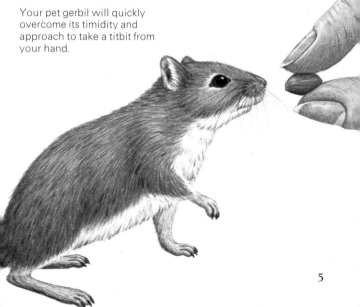

Breeds and colours

Breeds

Mongolian Gerbil This is the most popular breed. Any
gerbils in a pet shop will almost certainly be Mongolian
gerbils. An adult male is about 10cm (4in) and weighs
130g (4½oz); the female is a little smaller. It originated in
North-east China and is sandy brown in colour with a
paler abdomen. The fur on the feet is also lighter in
colour. There is a black line down the centre of the back
and the ears and tail are tipped with black.

Jerusalem Gerbil This breed is much larger than the
Mongolian gerbil and the fur has a hint of red. It differs
from other gerbils in that it is a solitary animal and the
males and females do not stay together after mating. It
appears more rat-like than the Mongolian gerbil and it is
more likely to bite. Consequently it is not a good pet.

Egyptian Gerbil Usually a light sandy brown but some
have a tint of red. It is a small variety, easy to tame and
groups will live together happily. It makes a good pet.

Libyan Gerbil This is the rarest gerbil to be kept as a pet.
It is much larger than the Mongolian gerbil, growing up
to 20cm (8in) in length, and has longer ears. It is more
aggressive and is difficult to breed as the females tend to
eat their young.

Indian Gerbil This is also known as the red-footed gerbil.
It is small with no hair on the tail and feet, which are a
deep pink. It dislikes company and as it is difficult to
tame it does not make a good pet.

Namib Paeba Gerbil This gerbil is less well known than
the other breeds. It is sometimes called the Snowshoe
gerbil because of the shape of its feet.

Prezwalski's Gerbil One of the largest gerbils at over 20cm (8in). It is more rat-like than other breeds and has thick coarse hair and a short hairless tail.

Gerbils are mostly the same size, but there are many different colours as shown by these cinnamon and black gerbils.

Fat-tailed Gerbil This North African gerbil is so called because of its short stumpy tail. It has light coloured hair and a white abdomen.

Great Gerbil As its name suggests, this is the largest of the gerbils. It is deep red and in the Soviet Union it is considered a pest because it damages crops. It is not a good pet.

The albino gerbil has a white coat and pink eyes. Typically, a gerbil has a sandy coat and black eyes.

Colour variations As gerbils have been domesticated for a relatively short period, there are not as many varieties to choose from as in other pets such as rabbits. However, new colour variations are being developed as they become more widely kept but normally only the Golden Agouti form of the Mongolian gerbil is available at pet shops.

Golden Agouti A golden red with black guard hairs, a white abdomen and a black tip to the tail. It has black eyes, black and white whiskers with light grey ears that have a golden edge.

White Spot or Canadian White Spot This has a normal sandy coloured coat with a white spot on the nose, forehead and neck. There are white feet and a white tip to the tail.

Pink-eyed White – Albino The gerbil has a pure white coat, white whiskers and pink eyes. The ears are flesh-coloured with white hairs.

Dark-tailed White Up to the age of 13 weeks this variety resembles an Albino, then a dark ridge appears on the tail, hence the name.

Argenti Golden all over with no guard hairs. The abdomen and feet are white and there are hairs on the ears. The eyes are red.

Black Jet black hair with black eyes, whiskers and ears.

Dove This gerbil is a soft grey colour with light grey whiskers and ears and red eyes.

Grey-bellied This can be any of the standard colours but it always has a grey abdomen.

Dilute The fur on the body is light golden shading to grey at skin level. In addition, there should be no dark hairs and no ridge on the tail.

9

Housing

Gerbils require a minimum temperature of 20-24°C (68-75°F), but they must not be exposed to draughts or to excessive heat even though desert animals, so do not keep them on a sunlit window sill. A wide range of housing is available for gerbils but in many ways the most easily maintained and the most entertaining for the owner is the gerbilarium.

An ordinary hamster cage can easily be turned into a home for your gerbil.

Cage furnishings should include a small non-tip food bowl and a gravity-feed water bottle. Ramps, ladders and branches can be provided to increase exercise space, and also cardboard tubes.

Wooden cages can be built, using hard wood to limit the damage from the gnawing habits of the gerbils. This damage can also be limited by ensuring that there are no exposed edges unless they are metal.

Rotastak One of the most satisfactory of the commercially available cages is the Rotastak. This is an elaborate system of interconnected, ventilated, round, plastic modules which imitate the burrow systems. Although expensive, the system allows easy cleaning and it is long-lasting and easily expandable. It is essential to use anti-gnawing rings on the exposed edges of the interconnecting tubes.

The Rotastak 'playroom' is a recent innovation. Gerbils are able to move from level to level through the tubes. Extra compartments can be slotted in when required.

Gerbilariums At its simplest a gerbilarium is an aquarium containing a deep enough floor material for the gerbil to be able to construct a network of tunnels. This tunnelling habit is common to many desert animals, the burrows enabling the animals to escape the heat of the day. To house a breeding pair of gerbils an aquarium measuring 60cm x 38cm x 30cm (24in x 15in x 12in) must be considered the absolute minimum. People often dispose of aquariums when they begin to leak, but this doesn't matter when keeping gerbils, and consequently a second-hand aquarium is often fairly cheap.

Fill it to a depth of at least 15cm (6in) with a suitable burrowing medium. Whilst a variety of different burrowing materials have been used, one of the most suitable is made from a mixture of equal parts of prepacked sterilized potting compost, moss peat and short-chopped straw; to this can be added a few handfuls

A gerbilarium with accessories. Before adding the gerbils, make sure there is at least 15cm (6in) of burrowing material.

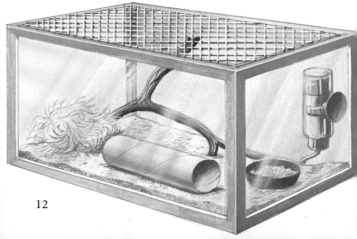

of activated charcoal to keep the mixture smelling sweet. This mixture should be placed in the gerbilarium and firmed down well before the animals are introduced. They will soon produce a gallery of tunnels which will provide the pair with security and privacy, and enable them to live as they would in the wild although on a much smaller scale. The gerbilarium must also be topped with a tight wire-mesh lid to prevent any escape.

The gerbilarium can be furnished with dried branches which have been scrubbed in hot soapy water and then well rinsed and dried, well scrubbed stones, a feed bowl and a water bottle. A nesting box will not normally be required for breeding because the gerbils will excavate their own nesting chamber within the burrowing material, but suitable nesting material will be required. A gerbilarium should not need to be completely broken down more than once every 3-4 months although any uneaten food should be removed daily to prevent it going stale.

Cages Many gerbils are housed in standard hamster cages – make sure, however, that they have a minimum of 1250 sq cm (200 sq in) of floor space for each breeding pair. The floor should be covered with layers of newspaper topped with a generous layer of sand, sawdust, woodchippings or peat, or a mixture of any of these substrates. Nesting boxes are unnecessary except immediately before an anticipated birth but nesting material must be provided and various materials are suitable: toilet paper, tissue paper, kitchen towels, hay and special bedding material from pet shops. Cotton wool and knitting wool should be avoided because they can cause intestinal impaction and death if eaten.

13

Accessories

Toys Gerbils are extremely active, inquisitive and playful animals with a surprising degree of innovative behaviour. Because of these characteristics, gerbils appreciate the provision of a wide range of playthings. Before anything is provided for the gerbil to play with, ensure that it is not poisonous if chewed and that it has no sharp cutting edges. A wide variety of toys can be provided from household articles, such as wooden cotton reels, cardboard tubes, terracotta flower pots and scrap paper. Many commercially produced toys are also available. Plastic budgie ladders can be used as well as other small toys meant for other animals.

The most commonly purchased item and in many ways the most appreciated by the gerbil is an exercise wheel. A number of different types are available, but when choosing one make sure that the back and the wheel are solid. A slatted running surface and an open back with spokes can easily cause broken legs and an amputated tail if the gerbil should slip.

A new development of the exercise wheel is the playball. This is a clear plastic ventilated sphere in which the animal is placed. The gerbil can be allowed to propel it around the floor or the ball can be mounted on a stand to allow it to rotate freely. Your gerbil will need time to become accustomed to the ball and it should initially be placed in it for only a few minutes, gradually building up to a maximum of 20 minutes in any one hour. It is important never to leave your pet inside the playball in direct sunlight because it will heat up like a greenhouse. All commercial playballs are made from non-toxic

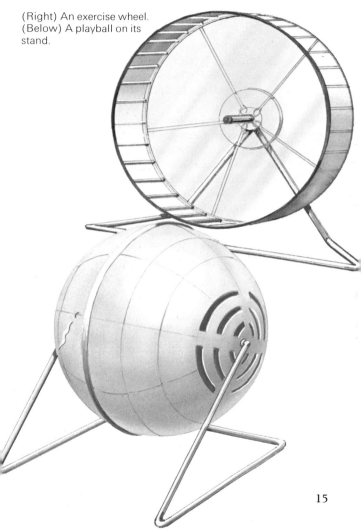

(Right) An exercise wheel.
(Below) A playball on its
stand.

materials and they should be washed in soapy water, rinsed and dried after use.

A recent introduction is a see-saw tunnel. This is made from a clear moulded non-toxic plastic tube with a narrow rubber ring set around the centre. The gerbil running through the tunnel will cause it to tip from side to side.

Nonchewable earthenware in the form of an old holey boot and a barrel can also be obtained.

Equipment One essential item is a wooden gnawing block since, because gerbils are rodents, their front teeth constantly grow and must be worn away by gnawing to prevent them becoming too long. Whilst any scrap of hard wood or pine can be used, in many ways it is safer

A cardboard tube, a wooden gnawing block and a bare cotton reel are simple items that your pet will enjoy enormously.

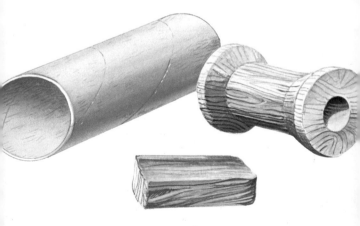

A sturdy food bowl and a
drinking bottle are both
essential pieces of equipment
for your pet gerbils.

to use the specially prepared 'wood gnaws' available
from pet shops. These wooden gnawing blocks are made
from *ochroma lagopus* wood which is non-toxic and hard
enough to ensure adequate tooth wear.

A range of drinking bottles and food containers are
available from pet shops.

When purchasing a water bottle, which will normally be of the gravity feed variety, ensure that it is
made from a good-quality easily cleanable material
(plastic is better than glass) and that it does not have too
great a capacity. In fact, a pair of gerbils only drink at
most 10-15 ml of water per day. The water should be
changed daily and the bottle sterilized weekly. Be careful
to ensure that the bottle does not leak and that it is not
positioned so that the gerbils could pile bedding up to
the level of the spout which will cause the bottle to
dribble.

Feeding bowls should be untippable and made in a
material that is easily cleaned and gnaw-proof such as
earthenware, which is best, or metal. Do not use them for
water as it may become dirty.

17

Handling

As with all small mammals, gerbils should be handled with great care, and young children should be supervised by an adult. They are easily tamed and feeding time presents an ideal opportunity to gain the animal's confidence. Allow the gerbil to eat food placed in an outstretched palm. After several days you can begin to stroke the gerbil with your other hand, ensuring that all movements are quiet and gentle.

If you handle the gerbil every day, you will eventually gain its confidence. You can then attempt to pick the animal up, either in cupped hands or by encouraging it to climb on to an outstretched hand. If frightened, the gerbil may jump from your hand and hurt itself, so always hold it over a cushion or other soft surface.

A gerbil can be held in cupped hands, but return it to its home if it is frightened.

Pick up the gerbil by supporting it in one palm while holding it at the tail's base. Never hold the tail's tip, which is very fragile.

Alternatively the gerbil can be picked up by the base of the tail and then placed on the palm of the hand, maintaining the hold on the tail. In many ways the easiest and most secure method is to place your palm over the animal's back and close the fingers under the abdomen, ensuring that the gerbil's head faces the wrist.

If handled for too long, a gerbil may suffer a collapse or fit; simply return it to the cage and allow it to rest. A gerbil will only bite if it feels insecure because of inexpert handling.

Feeding

Each gerbil will consume 10-20g ($\frac{1}{3}$-$\frac{2}{3}$oz) of food per day. A good basic balanced diet can be obtained from any pet shop. Alternatively you can mix your own including flaked maize, wheat, a few sunflower seeds and millet. Additionally you should supply small amounts of fruit and vegetables. Many gerbils enjoy small pieces of cheese, mealworms and raisins, but these should only be given as titbits. All vegetable material should be removed if it is not eaten by the end of the day. Oven-dried bread or bread soaked in milk will also be eaten but again these

A selection of gerbil delicacies: millet seed, sunflower seed, flaked maize, peanuts, slices of apple and carrot, a cabbage leaf and an ear of wheat.

should be offered as treats. Bacon rinds have been suggested as a food item but a number of problems have been associated with this.

Gerbils should be fed only once a day. If any food is left after 24 hours the amount of food provided the next day should be reduced slightly. Left overs should be removed from the cage, stale food being a possible cause of digestive upsets.

A variety of vegetables have been suggested as additions to the gerbil's diet. These include cabbage, cauliflower, lettuce, kale and broccoli in small amounts, plus parsley, celery, spinach and root crops such as carrot, swede, turnip, but do not ignore wild vegetation as a source of free food.

You must always be very careful, however, when collecting it to ensure that it has not been sprayed with poisonous chemicals and that it is not collected from the verges where it may be contaminated by car exhaust fumes. All wild vegetation should be washed and shaken dry before use. Dandelion, chickweed, dead nettles, comfrey, groundsel, clover and chopped young grass can all be fed.

Vitamin supplements may be obtained from pet shops, although they are probably unnecessary if you are providing a balanced diet for your gerbils.

Whilst it is said that gerbils do not require water it should always be available. Gerbils will only drink about 5ml of water a day but pregnant and nursing females may drink double this amount. They will certainly drink less than this if they are provided with greens and fruit. Water should be provided in a gravity feed bottle, and should be changed daily.

Cleanliness, hygiene and ailments

Cleanliness This is very important to your gerbil's health. They are very neat animals and will keep themselves clean but you must clean out the cage every fortnight adopting the following routine. (Gerbilariums are cleaned out less often.)

1. Clean out the substrate and bedding and burn or bury it.

2 Wash the cage with hot water and a mild disinfectant. Rinse and dry it thoroughly.

3 Clean and return the toys and accessories.

4 Add new substrate and bedding.

5 Never clean out a cage or gerbilarium housing

Young gerbils can easily be held in the palm of your hand, but always wash afterwards.

unweaned babies. If disturbed, the mother may panic and kill them.

Hygiene If your gerbil is ill, seek veterinary advice as soon as possible. Unfortunately, by the time the symptoms of many diseases of gerbils are recognized, it is often too late for successful treatment. The importance of hygiene in the handling of gerbils cannot be over-stressed, and anyone suffering from a cold or 'flu should not be allowed to handle a gerbil. The following rules should always be followed:

1 Wash your hands after handling the gerbil or cleaning out the cage.

2 Wash the gerbil's water bottle and food bowl separately from the household crockery.

3 The gerbil's food must be stored separately from the owner's food in sealable containers to prevent access to vermin.

4 Animals must not be brought into food preparation or storage areas.

5 Never eat or drink whilst playing with the gerbils or when cleaning out the cage.

6 Young children must be supervised by adults to ensure these rules are adhered to.

Ailments

Fits Some gerbils are affected by epileptic fits apparently caused by excessive handling or sudden changes in the diet or environment. There seems to be little or no long-term harm to the animals, but they should not be used for breeding because the condition may be inherited.

Scent gland disease Gerbils have a particularly well-developed scent gland in the mid-abdominal region. The area is hairless and tan in colour so that apparent bald patches here are normal. However, this scent gland can become infected and an abscess may form. If it does, cleanse the area with a salt or weak hydrogen peroxide solution.

Dental disease Because gerbils are rodents, the incisor teeth continue to grow throughout the animal's life. Only constant chewing will keep this in check. Any misalignment of these teeth or lack of opportunity for chewing can lead to overgrowth.

If this condition is ignored, the lower incisor teeth will continue to grow until they penetrate into the nose, and bleeding from the nose will be evident. A vet can periodically clip the teeth to keep this condition under control.

Ringworm This is relatively rare in gerbils. The symptoms are hair loss and scurfiness of the coat. This disease can be transmitted to anyone handling the gerbil and treatment is difficult, so the most responsible course is to put the affected gerbil to sleep.

Diarrhoea Symptoms are a wet tail and a soiled anus, and the droppings will be messy and smelly. Veterinary treatment should be sought. Diarrhoea is often the first symptom of Tyzzers Disease which can rapidly spread through a group of gerbils and is nearly always fatal. Food and bedding contaminated by wild mice droppings and urine being the usual source of infection, gerbils' food should be kept in sealed containers.

Heat exhaustion Even though the wild gerbil would seem able to survive the heat of the desert, this is only possible if they retreat into their deepest burrows during the intense heat of the day. They are usually active on the surface only in the morning and evening when it is much cooler.

Gerbils thrive best at 20°-25°C (68°-77°F) so it is important that the gerbil's cage is not left in direct sunlight. The gerbilarium usually contains insufficiently deep tunnels for the gerbils to escape the heat. If the animals in a cage or gerbilarium suffer from heat exhaustion, they should be transferred to a darkened room with the windows open. After making sure that the water bottle is filled, they should be left undisturbed until they recover.

In view of the large size and great weight of a gerbilarium, moving it would be difficult so it should be placed where heat exhaustion is unlikely to occur.

Colds The symptoms are continuous sneezing, runny eyes and a wet nose. The gerbil may also be lethargic and off its food. Colds are contagious so isolate the animal and leave it to recover undisturbed. As prevention is better than cure, keep the gerbil's cage warm and away from draughts.

Mange The most obvious symptom is a loss of fur resulting in large, bald patches. Mange is extremely contagious, and consequently the animal must be isolated immediately and treated with a commercial medication. The gerbil will also be low in vitamin C, so add a piece of an orange or other citrus fruit to its diet.

Wounds The most common cause is a fight with another gerbil. Bathe minor wounds in a very weak antiseptic solution. If the wound is deep, seek veterinary assistance as soon as possible.

Tail injuries Gerbils often lose the tips of their tails in accidents. No treatment is needed as the tail will normally heal by itself. However, it will not regrow.

Breeding

Whilst gerbils can successfully breed from as young as 6 weeks, it is better to delay the first litter until the age of at least 10-12 weeks. A maximum of 10 litters per year can be expected although some females may only produce 4-5 litters in a lifetime. Even though a gerbil can breed until it is 3 or 4 years old, it should be retired from breeding at about 18 months of age. If the gerbils are strangers, introduce them on neutral territory. If they begin fighting, separate them immediately but wear thick

Gerbils are difficult to sex. The male is slightly larger. Underneath, his rear is more tapered and there is a dark patch. The anal and genital openings are wider apart in the male.

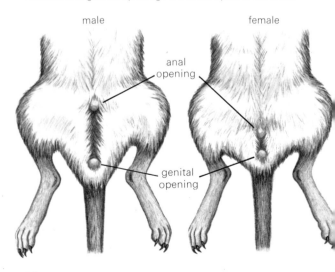

male

female

anal opening

genital opening

gloves when you do so, or you may be badly bitten yourself. You may then introduce them in the male's cage, but again separate them at once if they begin fighting.

Gerbils are prolific breeders, with the female coming into season every 4-5 days. The female remains on heat for only 4-5 hours normally during the evening when mating may well take place. The male shows his interest by drumming loudly with his hind feet and pursuing the female. The male will then be observed mounting the female, grooming, then mounting again in quick succession. The gestation period is about 24-26 days. Initially the female will show few signs of pregnancy but she will gradually gain weight so that by the time she looks obviously pregnant from about 20 days, she may well have put on 25g (1oz) in weight.

During pregnancy the female should be handled as little as possible and she should be offered extra protein in the diet. Ensure that water is always available because of her gradually increasing requirements. The male should not be removed from the cage during pregnancy or after the birth as he shares equally in the parental tasks. In the last week before the expected birth a small nesting box should be placed in the cage plus additional nesting material such as toilet paper or kitchen towels. This will ensure a degree of privacy and a darkened environment for the mother and young. An average litter contains four cubs although younger animals tend to produce smaller litters, as do females past their prime breeding age. A maximum of 12 cubs have been recorded.

In giving birth the female stands on her hind legs and

gently pulls the cubs out with her forepaws. The after-birth is eaten after being delivered in a similar fashion. The cubs which measure about 1cm ($\frac{1}{2}$in) and weigh about 3g ($\frac{1}{10}$oz) are born blind, naked and toothless. They are absolutely dependent on their parents and they may well be abandoned in the event of any human inter-ference during the days after the birth.

Cubs may be picked up in the mother's mouth much as a cat will pick up her kittens if they stray from the nest. Fur will be obvious on the cubs by 5 days of age and by 7 days they will have begun to explore the nest and this will be the earliest time that the nest can be examined.

A mother gerbil with two 3-week old cubs.

At birth, baby gerbils are totally dependent on their mother.

The cubs' eyes open at between 16 and 21 days. This is much later than other small mammals where it tends to be 7-10 days. The cubs should be weaned by 28 days and if as is usually the case the female has conceived again soon after birth, another litter will be due about this time.

From 6 weeks onwards the sexes should be segregated with the males being housed individually to prevent fighting. Gerbils are easily sexed at about 3-4 weeks of age, the male is usually larger and heavier than the female and his body also tapers more than the female's. A close examination under the tail will show that there is a much shorter distance between the anus and the genital opening in the female.

Exhibiting

Exhibiting gerbils is relatively new. In the United Kingdom the shows are organized by the National Mongolian Gerbil Society which sets the standards for judging gerbils. This society also issues newsletters and a yearbook.

Show gerbils should only be bred from proven stock and should be first class examples of their colour and

A standard show cage. Always make sure that there is some white shredded bedding paper to make the gerbil more comfortable.

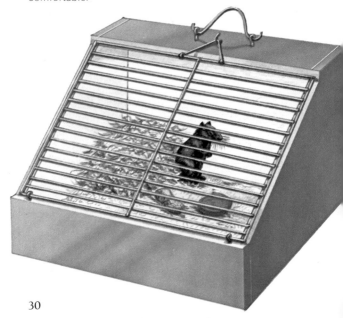

breed. Although close interbreeding is the best way to introduce new colour strains it also carries the risk of producing abnormalities and consequently selective breeding has become the more popular method.

Showing Like hamsters, gerbils are shown in a cage, the size of which is laid down by the National Mongolian Gerbil Society. The cages can be purchased from this source. A carrying box may also be needed if you intend showing gerbils some distance from your home. Food and water are usually allowed in the cage during the showing and judging of gerbils, but this should be kept to a minimum, as should be any bedding.

There are a number of things that the judge will be looking for and the gerbil will be awarded points on each of these.

1 The gerbil should be large, solid but not fat.
2 The tail must be at least as long as the body.
3 The head should be short and broad.
4 The limbs should not be too long or too short.
5 Eyes should be large and bright, ears small and erect.
6 The gerbil should be alert at all times and tame.
7 The coat should have a healthy sheen and there should be no bald patches or signs of moulting. The fur on the abdomen should be dense and not patchy. Points will be lost for any sores, scars or wounds, excess fat, bald patches or stained fur and also a dirty show cage. Disease will result in disqualification.

Index